SCHAUMBUR...

3 12   W9-BAH-917

THE ALCOHOLIC

VERTIGO
DC COMICS

"Last year I was at a storytelling event called The Moth, listening to Jonathan Ames telling a roomful of people a story from his life: funny and heartbreaking and much too personal for comfort. *The Alcoholic* is the comics equivalent of that: the kind of **odd, readable, painfully-honest**-even-if-we-don't-know-where-all-the-fictional-joins-are memoir-cum-fiction that could, a decade ago, only have been published somewhere out on the fringe of comics. Now it's right in the mainstream. I don't know how much Jonathan A is Jonathan Ames. I'm not sure I want to. But **I'm glad I read The Alcoholic."**

NEIL GAIMAN
author Sandman, American Gods

"*The Alcoholic* possesses that Amesian mixture of sexual and scatalogical hilarity with real horniness and also a tender humanity. **I went into a kind of spell reading this book.** I couldn't put it down. **Dean Haspiel's drawings are terrific, funny and immediate.** "

THOMAS BELLER
author The Sleep-Over Artist

"I fucking loved *The Alcoholic*! Ames has clearly researched his subject, and the result is **sometimes debauched, sometimes heartbreaking, hysterical and weirdly wholesome**. So good, it should be required reading at rehabs everywhere."

JERRY STAHL
author Permanent Midnight, I Fatty

THE ALCOHOLIC

JONATHAN AMES Writer
DEAN HASPIEL Artist

LEE LOUGHRIDGE Graytones
PAT BROSSEAU Letterer
Cover illustration: DEAN HASPIEL

JONATHAN AMES: For J.M.

Dean Haspiel would like to thank
Michel Fiffe, Sarah Butterworth,
Pedro Camargo, Kat Roberts,
and DEEP6 Studios.

Karen Berger Sr. VP-Executive Editor   Jonathan Vankin
Editor   Mark Doyle Assistant Editor   Louis Prandi Art
Director   Paul Levitz President & Publisher Georg Brewer
VP-Design & DC Direct Creative   Richard Bruning Sr. VP-
Creative Director   Patrick Caldon Exec. VP-Finance &
Operations Chris Caramalis VP-Finance John Cunningham
VP-Marketing   Terri Cunningham VP-Managing Editor
Alison Gill VP-Manufacturing   Hank Kanalz VP-General
Manager, WildStorm   Jim Lee, Editorial Director-WildStorm
Paula Lowitt Sr. VP-Business & Legal Affairs   MaryEllen
McLaughlin VP-Advertising & Custom Publishing John Nee
VP-Business Development   Gregory Noveck Sr. VP-Creative
Affairs Sue Pohja VP-Book Trade Sales Cheryl Rubin Sr. VP-
Brand Management Jeff Trojan VP-Business Development,
DC Direct Bob Wayne VP-Sales

THE ALCOHOLIC
Published by DC Comics, 1700 Broadway, New York,
NY 10019. Copyright © 2008 by Jonathan Ames and
DC Comics. All rights reserved. VERTIGO is a trademark
of DC Comics. Printed in Canada. First Printing.
DC Comics, a Warner Bros. Entertainment Company.
HC ISBN: 978-1-4012-1056-4
SC ISBN: 978-1-4012-1057-1

After the party, I walked home with my best friend, Sal. We had been best friends since we were two years old. It was also his first time getting drunk. We were really happy.

Before that night we weren't what you would call "nerds" but we weren't popular, either. We were in some kind of teenage, social-status limbo. Half nerd, half normal.

But drinking seemed to clear away the nerd part, at least for me.

My house, Ramapo, NJ.

LET'S GET DRUNK EVERY WEEKEND!

OKAY.

And that's just what we did--we got drunk every weekend for the next two years.

Sal and I had always been together. We had learned to do everything together.

We were Jonathan and Sal, Sal and Jonathan. The two names were said like they were one.

And now we were learning how to drink. But Sal could hold his liquor better and would always take care of me.

11

Later, I got sick. Real bad. Not because of what we had done--though maybe that contributed a little--but because of all the booze.

As always, Sal took care of me, washing me up, nursing me.

The next day, in the morning, even though we were hung over, we played basketball. Sal was taller than me, but I was the better athlete and I always beat him in sports.

We hadn't said anything about what happened.

After the game, we were just sitting on his driveway, silent. I was thinking that maybe we should go back in his house and try it again.

He was the first person I had ever touched.

Then I got the courage and was just about to suggest we go in the house, when he spoke first.

LET'S FORGET WHAT HAPPENED LAST NIGHT. IT WAS A MISTAKE. I HAD WONDERED WHAT IT WOULD BE LIKE WITH A GUY AND NOW I KNOW.

SO DON'T TELL ANYBODY.

OKAY.

AND LET'S NEVER TALK ABOUT IT AGAIN.

OKAY.

I was working up the courage to say something.

YOU EIGHTEEN?

YEAH.

So Sal and I never spoke again about that night, and we kept up our drinking. This one liquor store, before the drinking age was changed to 21, wouldn't card Sal because he looked pretty old.

And despite my destroying myself every weekend, I was still a good student and athlete.

I became editor of the school paper and I got varsity letters for fencing, tennis, track, and soccer.

I wrote a satirical article for the local paper, THE RECORD. It was about a syndrome affecting high school students who were wildly nervous about getting into good colleges.

They were doing way too much to have perfect, well-rounded applications, and in the process were losing their minds.

The affliction was called College Rejection Application Manifestation Phobia Syndrome.

DRUMBEATS

THE RECORD

C.R.A.M.P.S. ~ PLAGUING HIGH ACHIEVERS

BY JONATHAN A.

That article was very much about me--I was fifteen, sixteen, seventeen years old and was already leading a double life. Good student, good athlete, and good fledgling, vomiting alcoholic on the weekends.

I was trying, except for the drinking, to be perfect. It was my mom's dream that I get into a really good school, maybe in the Ivy League, and I was trying to make her dream come true.

I didn't really have my own dream. Not yet, anyway.

But then I read FEAR AND LOATHING IN LAS VEGAS by Hunter Thompson and something started waking up in my mind--the fantasy of being a writer.

HUNTER S. THOMPSON
Fear AND LOATHING IN LAS VEGAS

I started using "fear and loathing" for all my articles for THE RECORD and the school paper.

THE RECORD

FEAR AND LOATHING AT THE VIDEO ARCADE

by JONATHAN A.

Then I read Jack Kerouac, and he finished what Hunter Thompson had started. Now I had my own dream. Or, rather, I had Kerouac's dream, which probably wasn't much better than living out my mother's dream.

I wanted to be a writer who hitchhiked all over the country, having adventures.

But I didn't do any hitchhiking. I just went to parties and drank beer, thinking in my mind that I was like Kerouac.

Probably because I was doing well in sports and school, my parents had no idea about my drinking.

One night, I was so drunk that when I came home from a party I fell on the small set of stairs in our house and couldn't get up.

I heard my parents' door open-- it was around 2 a.m.--and my father called out my name. I couldn't get off the stairs and I thought I had been finally caught and I was relieved.

Some part of me WANTED my parents to figure out what I was up to.

JONATHAN?

AT LAST.

KLUTZ.

I couldn't believe it. He didn't for a moment think I had been drinking. He just thought I was uncoordinated. He had been calling me a "klutz" my whole life.

So I kept drinking, and for a long time, I was always thinking about what had happened with me and Sal, and I was always wondering if I should work up the courage to suggest we try it again.

But then I started meeting girls and I sort of forgot about fooling around with Sal.

We sometimes went on double-dates. This one night, I was on a first date with this girl from a nearby town. Her name was Stacy.

She was fifteen and I was seventeen. She had braces, but she was very pretty.

"HOT 'N JUICY

THAT'S ME! THAT PLACE IS ME!

WHAT DO YOU MEAN?

I LOVE HER!

"HOT AND JUICY!" GET IT? THAT'S ME! *HOT AND JUICY!*

18

Stacy and I, despite our less-than-perfect start, went out for almost two months. This was during my senior year of high school.

72 seconds.

But I was a lousy lover. I was too overwhelmed by how good it felt.

37 seconds.

11 seconds.

DON'T MOVE!

OKAY.

OH, SHOOT!

NOT AGAIN!

So then we tried oral sex. It was Stacy's idea.

Naturally, I was a little scared because of her braces.

But she didn't hurt me--she was very gentle.

I tried doing it to her, but she didn't like it.

STOP IT, I FEEL EMBARRASSED!

WOW!

Only one time did we--did I--manage to make love to her half-decently. We were in my tiny car, a 1979 Dodge Omni, and we were in the front seat and something about the angle made it work for us.

THIS FEELS REALLY GOOD FOR ONCE!

Soon after the good time in the Omni, there was a problem.

I HAVE SOMETHING TO TELL YOU. I KISSED SOMEBODY.

WHY?

HE WAS CUTE.

I broke up with her on the spot.

HOW COULD SHE? HOW COULD SHE?

It was around the time of my break-up with Stacy that something happened between Sal and me.

All my life I had been calling him and saying, "Whatta you wanna do," and he would say, "I don't know, whatta you wanna do?" and then I'd say, "I don't know whatta you wanna do?" And we'd go on like that for quite some time, but then...

HEY, SAL, WHATTA YOU WANNA DO?

OH, OKAY... TALK TO YOU LATER.

...he stopped playing the game on the phone and then stopped calling me altogether. He never wanted to hang out anymore. One day, I called him and the phone was busy for a while, so I decided to just walk over to his house and see what he was up to.

He was going somewhere. There were a bunch of kids in his car. His new friends.

I prayed that he didn't see me in the rear-view mirror.

Without there being a fight or anything said, somehow our friendship, after fifteen years, had ended.

Still, I kept hoping that Sal was going through a phase that he would snap out of. But, basically, he was giving me some kind of silent-treatment, which he broke only two times...

I was doing what I called a "Starsky and Hutch" maneuver. I destroyed my car and could have died. I was sober at the time.

I had done the same thing drunk a few nights before and nothing had happened.

So the first time Sal spoke to me in a while was after the accident.

I HEARD WHAT HAPPENED.

YEAH, MY PARENTS ARE REALLY UPSET. BUT CAN YOU BELIEVE I WASN'T EVEN DRUNK? I WAS PRETENDING TO BE STARSKY AND HUTCH.

I tried to pretend that it was normal for him to come see me, so I acted all casual about everything.

YOU SHOULDN'T JOKE ABOUT IT. YOU'RE A FUCKING IDIOT!

WHY? WHAT DID I DO WRONG?

YOU COULD HAVE DIED!

It was almost like there were tears in his eyes, but he ran away and wouldn't talk to me.

25

The next time we spoke, I was at a party and this girl that Sal liked got it in her head to give me a backrub in front of everyone.

Sal wasn't there, but right when she started the backrub, he showed up.

SAL!

SLAM

Because I destroyed my car, I was using my old ten-speed bicycle.

I found Sal at the diner in town, the *Phoenix*. He was smoking, which I had never seen him do before, and he was playing this sad Carole King song over and over.

He was hardly paying attention to me, but I was glad just to be with him.

I'M REALLY SORRY. I DON'T LIKE HER. SHE JUST WANTED TO GIVE ME A BACKRUB.

DON'T WORRY ABOUT IT.

We graduated from high school, and we didn't sit with each other at the prom, which broke my heart, but I didn't show it.

And then that summer, his family suddenly was moving to Chicago and Sal was going to go to the University of Illinois. I had been accepted to Yale...

I'LL WRITE TO YOU. I'LL COME VISIT YOU.

SURE.

GOOD-BYE, SAL!

All along I kept hoping that Sal and I would be friends again. At first, I wrote him letters every few months, but he never wrote back. So I stopped writing.

One time, I called his school and got hold of him, but he quickly got off the phone. I wouldn't see Sal again for six years.

I WAS STILL VERY DRUNK, SO THAT'S WHY I BURIED MYSELF LIKE THIS, THINKING THAT I WOULD BE HIDDEN, CAMOUFLAGED FROM THE POLICE.

Like I mentioned earlier, I went to Yale.

FEB. 18, 1985

Yale

CYRANO WINS AGAIN

WHY ARE YOU CALLED CYRANO?

THE COACH GAVE ME THAT NAME BECAUSE MY NOSE IS BIG. BUT CYRANO IS A GREAT SWORDSMAN. ALL THE GUYS ON THE TEAM ARE NAMED AFTER FAMOUS SWORD-FIGHTERS.

I LIKE BIG NOSES.

So I did all right at Yale. I had quite a few girlfriends, and I had my share of friends, but I was also something of a loner.

All my life, I've never really been a part of groups. What I do is have one-on-one friendships.

Sometimes, I wish I could be different in this regard, but it seems to be a trait almost like eye color--impossible to change.

I also drank a lot while in school; I liked going to the neighborhood bars in New Haven.

I went through a Hemingway phase and got into two bar fights. Hemingway said you should throw a left jab and a right cross. I followed that advice and won my first fight.

And I lost the second one.

After losing the fight, I dropped Hemingway and wrote a long paper on Jack Kerouac, returning to my high school hero.

My favorite writers are almost always alcoholic.

On the Road

I still vomited a lot from drinking, but not as much as I had in high school. I was getting better at controlling it, but, still, I probably vomited forty times in four years at Yale. That's not quite normal.

I was an English major and graduated in 1986 with a low C average.

My parents still didn't know about my drinking. I was afraid if they knew they would be terribly hurt and disappointed, so I hid it from them.

WE LOVE YOU, JONATHAN.

WE'RE VERY PROUD OF YOU.

I LOVE THE TWO OF YOU.

After school ended, I stayed in New Haven, working at the main library on campus. My goal was to be a writer, and I figured that working in a library was more or less ideal.

It wasn't the usual thing to do with a Yale degree, but my parents were supportive.

So I got an apartment in New Haven and started writing.

I also drove a taxi a few nights a week to bring in extra money.

WHAT?

NO! NO! NO!

Then the worst possible thing happened.

Just two months after graduation, my parents were in a terrible car accident and I lost both of them.

I only had one relative I was close to--my Great Aunt Sadie. All my grandparents were dead, and my parents, like me, had both been only children.

I had some distant cousins, but nobody that I was close to.

My Great Aunt Sadie was my mom's aunt. Ever since I was a little boy, she had been good to me.

My parents shared this big closet in their bedroom. I had to collect their clothes to donate them to charity.

I went on the longest crying jag of my life that day. I couldn't stop. I ended up asking a friend of my mother's to deal with their things. It was too much for me.

Holding their clothing, smelling traces of my mother's perfume and my father's cologne, it was almost like they were alive, but they were just beyond my grasp, elusive, gone, lost forever.

At first I kept on with my life, as if nothing had changed.

But I couldn't go a minute without this flash of pain across my mind. I would see them and then I would have this one thought that I would repeat over and over:

"You didn't love them enough."

It was sort of like OCD. The other thought I'd have is imagining their horrible pain right at the end, that their last thoughts were filled with terror.

I started driving down from New Haven to Queens on Sundays to visit my Great Aunt.

YOU SHOULD GO TO PARIS. I DID THAT WHEN MY FIRST MARRIAGE FELL APART. YOU'VE GOT TO PUT THIS BEHIND YOU.

41

So with some of the money I inherited, I went and lived in Paris. I sat in cafés and drank and wrote in my journal.

I tried to go to the places in Aunt Sadie's water-colors--Montmartre, the Luxembourg Gardens. I went for long walks by the Seine.

I got a French girlfriend, Amelie, and we smoked a lot of hash together.

Smoking hash wasn't in Aunt Sadie's watercolors, but I loved it.

I especially loved to get high and then nurse on her. I found it deeply soothing. She indulged me in this and she seemed to like it, too.

For a little while, I could forget what had happened.

AU REVOIR.

AU REVOIR.

After nine months, I left Paris and Amelie. For a few years we wrote letters and then we stopped. I'm not sure who stopped first. She was kind to me and I will never forget her.

I didn't come back with watercolors, but I came back with a lot of pictures.

The trip to Paris had been good. I wasn't having those repetitive thoughts nearly as much. Just a few times a day.

I returned to New Haven, and I didn't go back to the library, but I started driving the taxi again.

One night, in March of 1988, I picked up this older drug-dealer named Arthur.

We had hit it off in my cab--I had chauffeured him around to all the people he was dealing to--and then he invited me back to his place, said he'd give me stuff for free.

He had lost his driver's license, so he needed a cab to make his drops. He said we could make it a regular thing and he'd tip really well. I was considering it.

The coke made me all talkative and so I opened up to him.

MY PARENTS DIED AND I HAVEN'T BEEN THE SAME SINCE.

I HEAR YOU.

44

I was really out of it and he tried to have sex with me, but because of the coke, he couldn't do it.

I woke up in a garbage can. He had put me in there because at some point I had started vomiting.

Arthur wasn't a bad guy--he had tried to help me when I was throwing up--but waking up naked in that garbage can was a terrible thing.

When I got back to my place, I was incredibly frightened. I felt like if I didn't get some kind of help I would die.

On some level, I wanted to die, but another part of me, some survival instinct, was also kicking in.

NEW HAVEN HOSPITAL

I checked myself into the detox unit and after a week there, they were going to send me to a rehab.

I didn't have too many people in my life, only my Great Aunt, really. So I called her and lied to her, as a way to explain why I wouldn't be seeing her for a while.

I'M GOING TO FLORIDA FOR A FEW WEEKS, SO I WON'T BE ABLE TO COME TO QUEENS.

THAT'S ALL RIGHT. BUT CALL ME. WE'LL HAVE A TELEPHONE-ROMANCE UNTIL YOU'RE BACK.

OKAY. I LOVE YOU.

I LOVE YOU MORE THAN THAT.

CLK

I didn't like lying to her, but I didn't want her to know that I was in trouble. I didn't want her to worry about me.

47

After the detox, I went to a rehab in a woodsy, beautiful part of Connecticut.

SPRING HILL

It was good to be there. It felt like I was taking an old-fashioned cure. At Yale, I had read and loved Thomas Mann's THE MAGIC MOUNTAIN, his novel about a healthy young man, Hans Castorp, who goes to a Swiss-Alp tubercular sanitarium for a week to visit his sick cousin and ends up staying for seven years.

Well, for me, Spring Hill was kind of like that and I was Hans Castorp. I could just quit life for a little while.

I did some therapy at the rehab, which I enjoyed. It's embarrassing to say so, but I've always been pretty self-involved, but, nevertheless, this was the first time in my life that I was really talking about myself AND someone was listening.

EVEN BEFORE MY PARENTS DIED, I ALWAYS FELT LIKE A LONER. NOW IT'S WORSE.

I WAS A PART OF THINGS IN COLLEGE, LIKE THE FENCING TEAM, BUT REALLY, SECRETLY, I ALWAYS FELT SEPARATE, LIKE NOBODY COULD KNOW ME AND I COULDN'T KNOW THEM.

I UNDERSTAND. ON SOME LEVEL, WE ARE ALL UNKNOWN TO EACH OTHER.

My therapist's name was Dr. Wilson and she was very beautiful. I didn't know that therapists could be so attractive.

I'LL BE BACK IN A FEW WEEKS, I THINK. I LOVE YOU.

I LOVE YOU MORE THAN YOU KNOW.

I still felt bad about lying to Aunt Sadie, but I didn't know any other way. I didn't want to hurt her.

48

SO THAT WAS THE SPRING OF 1988 WHEN I GOT OUT OF REHAB, AND I FELT GOOD FOR THE FIRST TIME IN YEARS.

SINCE I WAS FIFTEEN, I HAD BEEN MAKING MYSELF SICK FROM BOOZE FOR NINE YEARS. THAT'S NOT TOO LONG FOR A LOT OF ALCOHOLICS, BUT EVERYBODY IS DIFFERENT. SOME ALCOHOLICS HAVE TO ABUSE THEMSELVES FOR FORTY YEARS BEFORE THEY QUIT--IF THEY QUIT AT ALL--AND SOME ARE ABLE TO STOP WHEN THEY'RE TEENAGERS.

UNFORTUNATELY, JUST ABOUT THE ONLY THING THAT WILL GET AN ALCOHOLIC OR A DRUG ADDICT TO STOP IS PAIN. A LOT OF PAIN.

WELL, I WAS 24 AND READY TO BE SOBER.

I DECIDED TO MOVE TO NEW YORK. I WOULD BE CLOSER TO MY GREAT AUNT AND I WAS GOING TO WRITE. I GOT A SMALL STUDIO IN THE EAST VILLAGE ON THIRD STREET.

I STILL HAD SOME OF MY INHERITANCE THAT I COULD LIVE ON, AND I FIGURED I COULD WAIT TABLES OR DRIVE A TAXI TO BRING IN WHATEVER ELSE I MIGHT NEED.

DR. WILSON HAD SAID I SHOULD GO TO AA--I HAD ATTENDED SEVERAL MEETINGS AT THE REHAB--BUT THAT WAS HER ONE SUGGESTION I DIDN'T FOLLOW. I DIDN'T HAVE ANYTHING AGAINST AA, I JUST FELT THAT I COULD STAY SOBER WITHOUT IT.

AROUND THIS TIME, I LEARNED FROM A HIGH SCHOOL ACQUAINTANCE THAT SAL HAD MOVED TO NEW YORK. I WAS GOING TO LOOK SAL UP AND FINALLY HAVE A TALK WITH HIM. I FELT LIKE I MUST HAVE HURT HIM TERRIBLY WHEN WE WERE GROWING UP AND NOW WAS MY CHANCE TO MAKE AMENDS, TO SAY THAT I WAS SORRY.

SO I HAVEN'T QUITE GOTTEN THE STORY UP TO THIS MOMENT IN THE SAND IN AUGUST 2001, BUT, WELL, I'M NEARLY THERE...

Sal was living over in Hell's Kitchen. He was listed in the phone book. I called him up and like it was nothing, as if no time had passed, he said I could come over. I was really nervous about seeing him.

...IT WAS A BAD CAR ACCIDENT, JUST A FEW MONTHS AFTER I GRADUATED.

I'M SORRY.

I told him about my parents and he was kind and sympathetic.

Then I went into a long speech of apology telling him I was sorry that I had driven him away.

I recalled dozens of little injurious things I had done over the years of our friendship and I apologized for them all. I brought up the girl who gave me the massage and said I was sorry about that.

...SO I'M REALLY SORRY FOR EVERYTHING I DID AND I JUST WANTED YOU TO KNOW THAT.

I talked for about ten minutes straight and he just listened.

And when I was done, he didn't, at first, say anything, but then...

EVERYTHING YOU SAID WAS BEAUTIFUL AND I APPRECIATE IT. BUT YOU GOT IT ALL WRONG. I WASN'T ANGRY WITH YOU. I'VE NEVER BEEN ANGRY WITH YOU. I DIDN'T CARE ABOUT YOU GETTING A MASSAGE FROM THAT GIRL.

I WASN'T JEALOUS OF YOU BEING WITH HER. IT WAS THE OTHER WAY AROUND. HER BEING WITH YOU. I WAS IN LOVE WITH YOU.

I REALIZED BACK IN HIGH SCHOOL THAT I WAS GAY. BUT I DIDN'T WANT TO DO ANYTHING WITH YOU AFTER THAT FIRST TIME. I COULD TELL YOU WERE MORE INTO GIRLS...I DIDN'T WANT TO WRECK YOU.

Sal had to meet some friends for dinner, but before I left his apartment we spoke of reviving our friendship and I felt really good. This shadow had been lifted from my life.

I could stop hating myself.

I kept thinking, though, about this one thing he had said: I DIDN'T WANT TO WRECK YOU.

About a week after our big talk, we had dinner and I learned more about Sal's life. He went out a lot and was barely able to keep up with his studies--he was in graduate school for architecture at Columbia.

I PROBABLY GO DANCING FIVE NIGHTS A WEEK. THERE ARE A LOT OF DRUGS, BUT IT'S COOL.

BE CAREFUL.

OF COURSE.

So much time had passed that it was like we were different people, especially now that I wasn't drinking, but I figured that in time we would be close again.

HI, SAL, IT'S JONATHAN. GIVE A CALL WHEN YOU CAN.

I called him a few days later and he didn't call back. So then two weeks after that I called him again. Then I called him a month later, and then two months after that.

Always I would leave some tepid message: "Just calling to say hi."

He never once called me back.

I had started reading a lot of Raymond Chandler and Dashiell Hammett and as a result, I started writing a mystery.

The narrator was a Jewish guy my age named Max Irwin. I named him after my father. My father's first name was Irwin, his middle name Max.

I reversed the names and he sounded tough and cool. And in the book, I was going to have Max Irwin save a woman named Florence--that was my mother's name.

Like in New Haven, I drove a taxi at night to pay my bills.

And that's the job I gave Max--driving a cab. One night a beautiful young woman comes in his cab and she needs his help, and to make a long story short, Max solves his first murder. The book was called: WHAT THE EYE DOESN'T SEE.

I found an agent and the book was published in 1990.

WHAT THE EYE DOESN'T SEE
BY JONATHAN A.
#044
THE COMPLETE BOOK
USA $5

The first time I went to a bookstore to find my own book was a great moment. I haven't really been proud of myself too many times in life, but that was one time when I felt pretty good, for a few minutes anyway.

I'm not making a grand statement one way or the other, but I've always disliked myself more than I've liked myself.

I wished that my parents could be with me in the store, but I did have my great aunt.

AT LEAST WE KNOW THERE'LL BE ONE SALE.

HE WROTE THIS. HE'S MY NEPHEW.

I was really hoping Sal would spot the book and contact me, but he didn't.

Over the next eleven years, I wrote five more "Max Irwin" books. After solving that first murder as a taxi driver, Max became a private detective.

The books did okay, and I was able to make a living. I also did some freelance journalism, and once in a while I taught a writing class at the New School.

1991

1994

1997

2001

As the years went by I was producing more books, but also losing more hair. I tried a number of things to reverse the process. I tried eating lots of seaweed. I tried giving up coffee. I tried a rubber scalp-invigorator. But it was all to no avail. My hair was disintegrating!

By 2001, I had this line of hair at the front that I let grow very long. I called it the "fringe" or the "hedge." It was made up of several filament-like hairs that I combed over my bald spot, which, for some reason, was at the front of my head, instead of the back. I called this styling a "comb-back," and hoped that it wasn't as disgraceful as a comb-over, though I've known several older Italian waiters who look quite good with their comb-overs.

In fact, I know one waiter, Sylvio, who combs a single hair from his left ear to his right ear.

Sylvio.

OTOGRAPHS

POSES $1.50

As the years went by there were four constants in my life--writing, not drinking, worrying about my hair, and visiting my Great Aunt Sadie on Sundays. We'd have lunch and play cards. We did this for years.

In 1989, when I was working on my first novel, WHAT THE EYE DOESN'T SEE, she was 79 and she had one of her breasts removed.

DO YOU WANT TO SEE THE SCAR?

OKAY...

I'm not sure why I wanted to see it--morbid curiosity, I guess.

THIS IS LIFE. YOU CAN'T BE SQUEAMISH.

She was trying to make me tough, but it didn't work.

My Great Aunt and I were very close, but sometimes we were too close.

For every holiday, Jewish or American--Passover, Thanksgiving, Yom Kippur (to break the fast), New Year's Day--my Great Aunt and I would go to this Greek diner on 108th Street, in her neighborhood, Rego Park Queens.

This diner catered to the older Jewish people in the neighborhood and would actually have Jewish food on the Jewish holidays. We were well known in that restaurant.

I LOVE EGG MATZO.

IT TASTES LIKE WALL-PAPER TO ME.

GREECE

As she got older, we would take naps on her two couches after we played cards. She always gave me her bed, which was the more comfortable couch.

HAVE A GOOD DRIMMEL.*

*Drimmel is Yiddish for nap.

Sometimes I couldn't sleep and I would just look at her.

1969

When I was little, my Great Aunt Sadie would take the bus out to New Jersey once a month and spend a weekend with us. She was very glamorous, like a movie star. I loved her visits.

For over fifty years, she worked as a manicurist in the best salons in New York. She had two husbands and many boyfriends. She was kind of a Jewish Holly Golightly.

JONATHAN, MY BEAUTIFUL BOY!

Because of a botched, illegal abortion when she was young, she couldn't have children. I was like the son and grandson she could never have.

I LOVE YOU, I LOVE YOU, I LOVE YOU.

When she would stay over, I'd get up early and sit by the couch where she slept in our house and wait for her to wake up. As soon as she got up, she'd play with me.

GOOD MORNING, SUNSHINE.

So then 30 years later, I was still watching her sleep, still loving her, still waiting for her to wake up.

And now I was the one who had to bend over to kiss her goodbye.

I LOVE YOU, I LOVE YOU, I LOVE YOU.

YOU NEED TO MASSAGE OIL INTO YOUR SCALP. YOU'RE TOO YOUNG TO BE THIS BALD. I HOPE YOU DON'T HAVE MANGE.

AUNT SADIE!

I LOVE YOU.

I LOVE YOU MORE THAN YOU KNOW.

It was always sad to leave her on Sundays. We had our rituals--she'd stand in the window and I'd wave good-bye to her.

Other than me, she hardly saw anyone. She was too proud to go to the senior citizen center--"I'm not that old," she'd say.

So that was my life for a number of years. I didn't drink, but there was a bar right next door to my apartment building in the East Village and every night when I'd pass it, I'd say to myself, "Maybe I should go in there."

But then I'd think about waking up in that garbage can and I knew if I drank, that something like that would happen again. It would only be a matter of time.

I knew that there was an urge in me for total oblivion and total destruction.

Then in 1998, I moved to Brooklyn, the Boerum Hill neighborhood, and right on my corner was this old, romantic bar. Every night I'd pass it, look in the window, and have that same desire to go in, just like with the bar in the East Village.

Along with part of me always wanting to drink, I was always keeping one eye open for Sal. I felt sure that some day he would show up at a book signing or I'd just run into him on the street.

So, for years, every day I thought about drinking and every day I hoped to run into Sal.

I courted her. We took things slowly. She was twenty-three and I was thirty-six. She was a year out of college and living with her parents in Manhattan, in the West Village.

To protect her identity, I'll call her Manhattan for now.

I'M OLD! I'M GOING BALD.

YOU'RE NOT OLD.

LOOK!

I STILL THINK YOU'RE ADORABLE, LIKE AN OLD DOG.

This age difference was a concern for me and for her, too, but we dealt with it by joking about it.

Manhattan was a talented graphic designer and a lover of books. That was the thing we had most in common--we loved to talk about what we were reading.

After two weeks, we had our first kiss, and as we kissed I thought that I wanted to marry her. I had never had that thought before in my life.

After two weeks of not talking, she called and left a message on my machine. To deal with the pain of her leaving, I couldn't call her, in my mind, by her name. So she became San Francisco.

But any time I saw "San Francisco" in the paper, like on the sports pages, which I read daily, it hurt terribly.

CALL ME, I MISS YOU.

I GOT YOUR MESSAGE, CALL ME ANY TIME, LATE, I DON'T CARE. YOU CAN WAKE ME UP. IT WAS GOOD TO HEAR YOUR VOICE.

She didn't call back. This started a disturbing trend that lasted the next few months--she would call when she knew I wasn't home and leave a message.

I would call back, leave a message, and then she wouldn't return my call.

November 2000.

February 2001.

So this went on and on.

78

HELLO?

HI, IT'S ME.

WILL YOU MARRY ME? I LOVE YOU.

She hung up. I was insane! I had planned to tell her off and I did the opposite!

JULY 2001.

Then I heard that she had a boyfriend in Seattle and moved there to be with him. Her third city in nine months.

YOUR PENIS IS BEAUTIFUL AND HUGE--SO MUCH NICER THAN JONATHAN'S.

I began to have the most obvious dreams. I was still in love with her. But it was that French love--amour fou. Crazy love.

Wherever I went, even though I knew she was now in Seattle-- why was she moving around so much?!?--I kept expecting to see her in New York. I thought about her nearly every second of every day.

WHERE'S SEATTLE? WHERE IS SHE?

FEET OFF THE CUSHION!

SORRY.

I needed to do something after my relapse on the booze. So I went out and got a pair of clippers. Who was I fooling with my comb-back? No one!

But my impulse was mostly borne out of self-loathing--I wanted to injure myself in some way, punish myself.

As soon as my hair was gone, I regretted shaving it off. But to grow back my fringe to a length where I could perform my comb-back would take months, and an in-between phase, with a fringe that didn't reach all the way to the back of my head, would look ridiculous.

I was going to have to keep shaving it.

A BEER, PLEASE.

WHAT KIND?

WHATEVER YOU HAVE ON TAP.

I had thought, at first, that I would just get sober again, but the booze had gotten into my skin, my psyche. I had felt some relief that day in Asbury Park.

It was the relief of oblivion.

So for the first few weeks, I reveled in drinking again. I was getting drunk five out of seven nights, but nothing too disastrous--like fleeing from policemen in Asbury Park--had occurred.

I felt like I was controlling it, that maybe I wasn't an alcholic.

I discovered that if I drank vodka I wouldn't get hung over. This was a great revelation and seemed to explain, to me anyway, the high rate of Russian alcoholism.

VODKA SODA, PLEASE.

After a night of drinking I would sometimes feel compelled to call Seattle. The city and the person. Then some sober brain-cell would force me to hang up the phone.

She had crushed my heart and testicles, but I still loved her.

Many nights after being in the bars, I would be overtaken powerfully by the sudden and imperious need to go to the bathroom.

OH, NO! NOT AGAIN.

I would make it home just in time. I felt quasi-heroic in these moments, like I had defused a bomb, saving the world, but I also felt rather pathetic, as you can imagine.

Once or twice, I have to admit, I didn't make it back in time.

So I was really losing it--my brain was shot with obsessive love-thoughts, I was back on the booze, and I was practically incontinent.

One night, I went to this bar where this old friend of mine, Bill, was the bartender. He was an ex-con and I often tapped him for information for my novels.

He had spent five years in prison for dealing drugs, but don't get the wrong idea--he was also a painter and quite a sweet guy.

WHAT HAPPENED TO YOUR HAIR?

BUZZED IT OFF. WAS LOOKING RIDICULOUS. CAN I HAVE A VODKA SODA?

I THOUGHT YOU DIDN'T DRINK.

I FELL OFF THE WAGON.

YOU SURE ABOUT THIS?

I chewed his ear off about Seattle.

SO SHE NEVER CALLS ME BACK, AND YET I DREAM ABOUT HER ALL THE TIME AND WHEREVER I GO I'M LOOKING FOR HER, EVEN THOUGH SHE'S IN SEATTLE.

I THOUGHT YOU SAID HER *NAME* WAS SEATTLE.

WHEREVER SHE LIVES, THAT'S WHAT I CALL HER.

SO WHAT DO YOU MAKE OF THE WHOLE SITUATION?

IT'S SIMPLE. YOU'RE HER BITCH.

ON THE INSIDE, YOU DON'T HAVE A CHOICE WHEN YOU'RE SOMEBODY'S BITCH, BUT YOU'RE ON THE OUTSIDE. SO WHEN YOU'RE READY, YOU CAN STOP BEING HER BITCH.

BUT YOU MUST LIKE IT.

Bill gave me his pipe and told me to go smoke some pot in the bathroom. He said that the marijuana, a healing herb, would help with my heart and my ass (my IBS).

I'M HER BITCH! I'M HER BITCH!

I felt that Bill's assessment of my situation was spot-on. I didn't know how to change it, but at least I had it spelled out.

I hadn't been stoned for years and I loved it. I was watching the drips of water on the beer-tap and they were the most beautiful things I had ever seen.

Then the pot hit me bad, and I couldn't lift my head and I felt like if I moved I would vomit all over the place.

TO MIX THINGS UP, I THOUGHT THAT RATHER THAN READ FROM MY NOVEL, I WOULD READ THIS ESSAY I WROTE A FEW YEARS AGO...IT'S RELEVANT TO WHAT I'VE BEEN GOING THROUGH LATELY...

I WANT TO SAY, BY WAY OF INTRODUCTION TO THE ESSAY, THAT I HAVE FOUND THAT THE WORLD IS DIVIDED BETWEEN THOSE WHO LIKE SCATOLOGICAL HUMOR AND THOSE WHO DON'T. FOR THOSE OF YOU WHO DON'T, PLEASE SEE THIS ESSAY AS A STORY OF HUBRIS, AN EXCESS OF PRIDE.

AND FOR THOSE OF YOU WHO LIKE SCATOLOGICAL HUMOR, I WILL NOW READ "I SHIT MY PANTS IN THE SOUTH OF FRANCE."

I read them this story of how when I was nineteen I went to the south of France with a friend from Yale. We were there to take a French course.

One night I was very drunk and bought a tuna fish sandwich from a CLOCHARD, which is French for bum. I bought it right off his hand, where it was resting SANS napkin.

It was late at night. All the cafés were closed.

After five minutes in my system that sandwich exploded. We were racing back into town, where we hoped one café was still open.

I'M NOT GOING TO MAKE IT!

Part of the essay was also about my experience with a colonic in 1997.

After the colonic, which I enjoyed, something went wrong.

OH, GOD!

The colon-hygienist forgot to tell me to go directly home, that after a colonic you need to be near a toilet for several hours!

There was a big wet spot on the seat of my pants, looking like a Rorschach blot, and I deciphered its simple psychological message: You're a loser!

The essay went over very well. I didn't tell them about my current state of near-daily incontinence, but by regaling them with these two earlier embarrassing incidents was sort of a way to confess.

HA HA HA

After the reading some fans took me out drinking. I got really drunk and played the maudlin fool. It's embarrassing to think about.

I'M IN LOVE WITH THIS GIRL. I CALL HER SEATTLE. I'M HER BITCH.

Then I went to see Bill.

I DID THIS DRAWING OF MY BALDING PATTERN.

YOU REALLY CAPTURED YOURSELF. YOUR NOSE IS HUGE.

THANKS.

I GOT A BUNCH OF COKE. WANT SOME FOR YOUR NOSE?

SURE.

I did coke for a few hours with Bill. Then I came home and took Tylenol PM, upon Bill's recommendation, but I couldn't sleep. I was frightened and freaked-out and terrified. The usual post-coke reaction.

SNFF

RRRNNGG

9:00 AM

OH, MY GOD.

A friend of mine called me to tell me what was going on. It was September 11, 2001.

I never watch TV, but I had an old one in the closet.

The whole thing was like Orson Welles's WAR OF THE WORLDS. As the news flashed that the Pentagon had been hit and that another plane had crashed, it felt like the world was coming to an end.

After the second tower collapsed, I went to the roof of my building and I could see the smoke in the distance.

ARE YOU ALL RIGHT?

SOME PEOPLE IN THE NEIGHBORHOOD ARE GOING TO GIVE BLOOD, THEY'VE ASKED ME TO JOIN THEM.

BE CAREFUL! I LOVE YOU.

I LOVE YOU.

A bunch of writers in my neighborhood got together and we all went to the Hyatt where the Red Cross was set up to take blood.

But I still had coke in my system and maybe marijuana, too. I didn't know what to do--how could I, in front of these other people, refuse to give blood and confess to doing drugs?

And if I gave blood would it hurt someone to get coke-tainted TYPE A?

As it turned out, they couldn't take any more blood--so my own little self-centered crisis was averted.

In the lobby of the hotel, I spotted the famous author John Updike. I had seen him in Brooklyn before. It was somehow reassuring that a great writer was there.

John Updike

And Updike had just given blood. That's all anybody could think to do. Give blood. And, that, as we all know, turned out to be futile on 9/11. The blood wasn't needed. There were hardly any injuries, only fatalities.

I hadn't slept in 24 hours. Finally, in the afternoon, I passed out.

After sleeping for a few hours, I went back up to the roof.

JONATHAN, CAN YOU HELP ME? MARK WAS IN WINDOWS ON THE WORLD. I NEED TO GO TO THE CITY AND FIND THE MORGUE. WILL YOU COME WITH ME?

YES... OH, MY GOD...OF COURSE.

My neighbor's name was Ellen. Her baby was six months old. Her husband, Mark, a stockbroker, had filled in for a colleague at the last minute at some meeting in Windows on the World.

All of her family and his family were in Long Island--no one could get to her, the city was shut down, and so that's why she asked me to go with her into Manhattan. She got a neighbor to look after her baby.

Somehow the A train was still running.

Ellen felt like she had to do something, and the only thing she could think of was to find her husband's body, to see him one last time.

She was certain he was dead.

She had heard that a temporary morgue would be by the old warship, the Intrepid--I don't know where she heard this, but there was no morgue there. The city was empty--no cars, a few scattered people here and there.

GO TO BELLEVUE--THAT'S WHERE THEY'RE BRINGING THE BODIES.

We started walking east towards Bellevue. I remember we passed a restaurant where some people were outside eating. It was so strange, the world seemingly had come to an end, and yet some restaurants were still open.

It was like people dancing as the Titanic went down. What else was there to do?

Like that movie, ESCAPE FROM NEW YORK, there was one cab drifting around. I've now mentioned WAR OF THE WORLDS and this movie, ESCAPE, because I have no other frame of reference in my sheltered life--other than fiction --for how things were on that day.

We got the taxi and the kindly driver took us to Bellevue. He wouldn't accept our money.

Mary, our sweet neighbor, had dutifully been baby-sitting.

We had been neighbors for four years, but I had never been in Ellen's apartment before. I looked around--this is where Mark had lived. He would never return.

THANK YOU, JONATHAN.

I CAN STAY ON YOUR COUCH, IF YOU LIKE.

THAT'S ALL RIGHT. I'LL BE OKAY. MARY IS GOING TO STAY WITH ME.

As I left her building, I flashed in my mind to Mark.

Over the years, we had waved hello and acknowledged each other, usually when he was on his way to work, but that was it.

He had called Ellen as he and others tried to make their way to the roof. He only spoke to her for a second before getting cut off, but he had said, "They'll save us on the roof."

On September 12th, like the rest of the country, I spent most of the day watching the news.

HELLO?

YES, I'M OKAY...

It was Seattle.

I WISH I HAD DIED...

It was kind of her to call. She said she had tried the day before but all the circuits had been busy. We didn't speak long. There wasn't much to say.

After we hung up, I had the morbid, self-centered thought that if I had somehow been at the World Trade Center, that now she would love me.

I quickly chased that thought from my mind.

On September 10th, I was reading an essay about incontinence and passing around a diagram of my balding pattern--my life, I felt, couldn't be more frivolous and ridiculous and meaningless.

And as the world came apart at the seams, I didn't even have the fortitude not to drink.

I haven't really talked about politics in this tale, because I've always been somewhat apolitical, in much the same way that I'm agnostic.

But here's how I would summarize my general world-view: resigned, defeated, and heartbroken.

My usual stance is: "I'm wrong and you're wrong." I don't think anybody knows what the hell is going on. It's all too confusing.

When I first got sober, though, at the age of 24, I became a vegan and was deeply concerned about the environment, that was my one political issue.

I felt guilty driving a cab, and I saw every car and its engine as a small fire that was burning everything up.

But then at some point I sort of just gave up in my mind. I did little things like recycle my plastic bottles and send 10 dollars to Greenpeace, but in my heart, I felt like it was a losing battle.

Man was too destructive, too lost. He would always be at odds with himself and with nature.

It's perhaps too apt a metaphor, but collectively man was like a gigantic alcoholic--he knew better but he couldn't help but destroy himself and everything around him.

My little detective novels were my fantasies--where justice could prevail, though always just barely, and usually at great cost.

So 9/11 confirmed my truest feelings about man--that we were hopelessly imbalanced, that suffering and destruction would always rule.

Ellen was up there alone with her baby. Her life was shattered.

I had no hope for the world, but that doesn't mean I didn't somewhere inside still have hope for my own little life, except all that hope was centered insanely on one person.

THANKS FOR CALLING ME TODAY... I APPRECIATE IT...BYE...YOU DON'T HAVE TO CALL ME BACK...I HOPE YOU'RE ALL RIGHT...I ADORE YOU ...BYE...

As always, I left a message. I tried not to slur my words.

On September 13th, I walked across the Brooklyn Bridge and went to Union Square in Manhattan.

There were no cars south of 14th Street, the city was under martial law. I walked down University Place and saw a huge crowd up ahead.

EXCUSE ME, DO YOU KNOW WHAT'S HAPPENING?

CLINTON IS HERE, HE'S GOING AROUND HUGGING PEOPLE.

The next day, September 14th, 2001.

OH, NO!

The girl in charge of reunions for my high school class tracked most of us down and let us know that a classmate of ours had died in the Trade Center.

I remembered sitting next to the boy in math class. He was famous for his freckles and his sweet nature. He had helped me with algebra-- he was better at it than me.

WHAT'S THE ANSWER TO NUMBER TEN?

We played tennis together a few times.

He had been sitting at his desk when one of the planes plowed through his office.

After I read the mass e-mail from the high school girl, there was a private one-on-one e-mail from her just for me.

OH, GOD. I CAN'T BELIEVE IT.

She knew I was friends with Sal and she had learned from someone else in our class that Sal was living with his parents in Illinois and that he was dying.

THANKS FOR LETTING ME KNOW, I'M GOING TO CALL HIS PARENTS.

She put her number in her e-mail and I called her and she told me that Sal had AIDS and that he hadn't responded well to the medications. So he had gone off the drugs and now he was dying.

She got all this from a girl that Sal had once dated, the only person from our high school that he had stayed in touch with.

When Bill's bar closed, it became an after-hours joint and the drugs came out. I'd give him a little money, but he didn't seem to want much.

I was really losing control. I started doing that classic thing of waking up each day and swearing that I would stay sober and by nighttime I'd be in a bar, and by the end of the night I'd go to Bill's.

COKE IS FOR SHARING.

So I'd wait for my turn to snort a line. I was hungry for the stuff. I felt like a rat.

As I would do the coke, I'd think of those tests they did, where rats would keep going back to the cocaine dropper until they died.

I didn't really even like the stuff. I liked the first line, maybe, and then after that you just had to keep doing it.

Sometimes when I would do the coke, I would dig inside myself, trying to remember if I had ever been happy.

Maybe it was the drugs, but I'd go through my whole life and I'd come up with nothing.

The next day, I would try to clear all the coke residue out of my nose with a netti pot, this yoga thing I had that flushes your nostrils with salt water.

After bingeing, I'd be obsessed with detoxifying myself.

I started going all the time to the Russian baths, which have been around for over 100 years.

RUSSIAN-TURKISH BATHS

RUSSIAN-TURKISH BATHS

They have steam rooms, a sauna, and the Russian room--which is like a furnace. It gets up to 200 degrees in there.

It was classic alcoholic behavior--I would tear down and then build up. I was playing out my own little repetitive Phoenix myth.

The problem with the baths is they made me feel a lot better. So good that I would start the whole mad thing over again.

I was trying to keep my life together, to not lose myself completely so I kept going, even if I was hung over, to see Aunt Sadie.

YOU LOOK TERRIBLE. WHAT'S THE MATTER?

I HAVEN'T BEEN SLEEPING WELL.

110

Getting out of the city for a month seemed like a good idea--to get away from the despair of 9/11, and, also, I could use my time in the country to sober up.

I was a bit concerned, though, that Dean Wilcox hadn't read my books. All my novels have a strong undercurrent of sex.

What if Dean Wilcox actually read one of my books? I wasn't the most appropriate choice for an all-girls school.

SWEETLEAF COLLEGE

THE KEY TO WRITING IS FINDING A SUBJECT THAT YOU'RE IN LOVE WITH.

They put me in a little house on a hill, overlooking the athletic fields. I loved watching the girls in their little field-hockey skirts.

But the whole thing was deeply absurd--it was like the setup for a pornographic horror film. My little house on the hill was like the PSYCHO house.

It was early October--we had started bombing Afghanistan, and there I was surrounded by hundreds of girls. It seemed like a safe place to be during a time of war. I wrote a little short story about it called "Womb Shelter."

YOUR DESCRIPTION OF THAT EVENING SKY IS VERY LOVELY. YOU'RE AN EXCELLENT WRITER.

THANK YOU, MR. A.

I was enjoying my job.

So the first week went well--I was staying sober and no one on the campus had actually read any of my books. I was safe! I still hadn't written my letter to Sal, but I was gearing up for it.

Then one night...

WE WANT TO PROPERLY WELCOME YOU TO SWEETLEAF.

SURE, YES, COME IN...

DO YOU WANT WINE OR BEER?

ACTUALLY, I'M ON THE WAGON, BUT FEEL FREE-- ENJOY.

One of the girls, a dear thing, had some pot, and it was very convenient that the couch turned into a pull-out bed.
...SO CLINTON SHOOK MY HAND...
...SO THAT'S THE STORY. I LOVE HER. I CALL HER SEATTLE NOW. SHE'S JUST A LITTLE OLDER THAN YOU GIRLS.
SHE SOUNDS LIKE A BITCH.
NO, I'M HER BITCH.
YOU'RE CRAZY!
I wasn't man enough for five girls--I don't know who is--but I did get to grab them quite a bit, and we all fell asleep in a wild, loving gigantic spoon.
It was twelve noon when I finally woke up.
RING
OH, HELLO, DEAN WILCOX.

I was fired and told to leave immediately. Word had spread to Dean Wilcox that I had held an orgy with ten girls. It was a small campus, and the girls had talked.

Somehow during the "orgy" one of my shoes disappeared. I had to flee Virginia with only one shoe.

That to me seemed the most symbolic aspect of it all. I was completely out of control. I had lost a shoe!

A few hours before.

THIS IS DISGRACEFUL! NOTHING LIKE THIS HAS EVER HAPPENED BEFORE.

I'M SORRY.

WHY ARE YOU ONLY WEARING ONE SHOE?

I DON'T KNOW.

When I got home there were no messages from Seattle. It looked like it was finally over.

I didn't blame her for anything. She was young and confused. What was my excuse? I was old and confused. I was sick to want it, but I wished she had called.

A few days after I got back, I was part of a large group-reading. It was to raise money for several of the decimated New York City firehouses. Back then there were many such fundraisers.

Monica Lewinsky was friends with one of the other writers and so she was there. It was very nerve-racking to read for her. After Clinton himself, she was the most famous person I had ever been around.

She's kind of the American Princess Diana.

IT'S VERY NICE TO MEET YOU.

I HAVE ONE OF YOUR BOOKS BY MY BED. BUT I HAVEN'T STARTED IT YET.

It was so strange that I had met Clinton, and now I was meeting Monica Lewinsky!

And she had one of my books by her BED! I was flattered.

I tried not to, but I couldn't help myself--I stared at her mouth.

YOU COMING TO DINNER? WE'RE ALL GOING TO THIS PLACE I HAVEN'T HEARD OF CALLED VESELKA.

SURE. I LOVE VESELKA. IT'S UKRAINIAN.

I wanted to tell her my Clinton story, to let her know that I understood, first-hand, his massive charisma and that I empathized, but I didn't think it would be appropriate.

KGB BAR

Cucina

The next day.

The coke was carving me out, gutting me.

OKAY. I'LL GO. I'LL STOP USING. I'LL GET SOBER.

So I called my old rehab and was able to speak to my counselor, Dr. Wilson, who was still working there. She told me that I could turn things around if I went to AA.

I planned to go to some meetings, but before I could get myself organized and contact AA, another strange opportunity presented itself.

A men's magazine was doing a big section on out-of-the-way travel places in the Americas, as a sort of antidote to 9/11, and yet again a writer had dropped out at the last moment. So I was offered a trip to Bequia, a small island in the Grenadines.

It took a plane and a boat to get there. I had plenty of time to think.

Why was I alcoholic? I can't blame my parents, but they contributed a little. My father was something of a fearful man, and part of my love of drinking and doing drugs is the loss of fear, of being out of control and not caring. It's a way to not be my father, to not be a fearful man.

And my mother was a perfectionist and I could never really live up to her standards, at least in my mind, and so drinking always felt like a relief--I didn't have to be perfect anymore.

And then, nothing to do with my parents, there has always been this germ of self-loathing in me, this desire deep down to destroy myself.

I read this line in a book once: "Alcoholics think they're bad and deserve to be punished."

Plus, there is the physical side to alcoholism, the allergy part--I've almost never been able to stop at one or two drinks. Once I get a taste for booze or drugs, I simply want MORE.

And I've never wanted to be a social drinker. I've just wanted to drink and not get in trouble, not feel in pain afterwards.

But there's always pain, because as Tony, my old friend from rehab said, you can't stay intoxicated forever. Eventually you come down and your body feels destroyed.

And for me there's also this terrible guilt. A feeling of shame for what I've done.

I once saw something in a book about the "sin of destruction," and that must be what I feel guilty about—that I've sinned against myself, against the part of me that doesn't want to die. The part of me that doesn't hate myself.

IS THAT SEATTLE? HAS SHE COME HERE LOOKING FOR ME?

No matter where I went I was looking for Seattle, longing for her.

My room in the little bed and breakfast was a bit rugged. I liked it very much. It was the first time in my life that I slept under a mosquito net.

One night, I dreamt about Sal. As always, when I dreamt of him, we were friends again.

Sal looked like a teenager and we were playing basketball across the street from where I lived in Brooklyn. In the dream, I had forgotten that he was sick.

I'M REALLY HAPPY TO SEE YOU.

ME, TOO.

The next day, I tried again to write Sal.

I was struggling to find the right words. I wondered if shortly after we saw one another back in 1988 that he learned he was sick.

Maybe that's why he never returned my calls--he had been ashamed, the early stigma of AIDS.

DEAR SAL,

I found my way back to the marina, where there was an old pay phone.

I dialed Seattle's number. I was so high that it felt like a real conversation.

I LOVE YOU. I REALLY DO. I'M SORRY I'M TOO OLD FOR YOU. SOME MEN TRIED TO KILL ME. I MADE A FRIEND NAMED DESMOND AND I LAY IN THE SAND AND MY BODY WAS SAND AND THE SKY WAS SAND...

When I got home there was an e-mail from the high school reunions girl.

Sal died while I was in Bequia.

I had never written the letter. I would never see or speak to my best friend ever again.

JONATHAN, THESE ARE MY PARENTS.

NICE TO MEET YOU.

THANK YOU FOR LOOKING AFTER ELLEN THAT FIRST NIGHT.

I WISH I COULD HAVE DONE MORE.

I CAN'T TAKE ANYBODY ELSE DYING. I THINK I'M CRACKING UP.

I spent hours at the Brooklyn Inn. The next morning I was puking.

HOW ARE YOU FEELING? YOU DON'T SOUND GOOD.

NOT GREAT, BUT I'VE BEEN WORSE.

I'M WORRIED ABOUT YOU. I'LL COME OUT TO QUEENS IN A FEW DAYS. I HAVE TO WRITE THIS TRAVEL PIECE ABOUT BEQUIA.

DON'T WORRY ABOUT ME. IT'S MY JOB TO WORRY ABOUT YOU.

By the end of the day, I felt better, which is always a curse. When you're hung over or coming off coke, you're sure you'll never use again.

But then your health starts to come back and you get it in your head that a drink would taste awfully nice.

The VILLAGE VOICE had called me. There was a transsexual pageant taking place at a midtown club.

The whole world was on fire and I was covering a tranny pageant. I had written about the transsexual world in my novel THE THIRD SEX.

I was standing next to a guy and a foil packet fell out of his coat. I knew it had to be drugs of some kind.

Somehow he didn't notice!

I was a bit drunk and a mad instinct came over me.

The next day around 4 p.m.

The heroin put me in an odd sleep for about eight hours. Then I left Carmen and went to the Russian baths.

I called a friend of mine in LA, an ex-junkie and a successful screenwriter. I told him what happened.

WELL, YOU'RE A MAN NOW. YOU'VE DONE YOUR BAR MITZVAH DRUG.

He made light of it, which helped a little--made me laugh. But he was also concerned for me. Very concerned. He said I should go to a detox and then rehab. But I didn't want to do that.

So, instead, I sweated for hours.

It's always the same with me--I poison myself and then I desperately want the poison out of me. I try to kill myself and then I try to save myself.

I had been gone for about 48 hours. There were many messages on my answering machine.

I listened to all the messages--my Great Aunt Sadie had fallen and broken her arm and her ankle. She was in a hospital in Queens.

She and the social worker at the hospital had been trying to reach me for two days.

And it was the same thing with alcohol: I had never stopped wanting to drink, even during the years I was sober.

My ego never wanted to accept that I couldn't handle the stuff.

My ego wanted me to be a hard-drinking writer, a romantic figure.

But I had to see that there was nothing romantic about my drinking. And it was getting worse--I had tried heroin and liked it.

And I had let down the one person who needed me--my great aunt.

I had wanted Sal's friendship and I had wanted the love of the girl and I had wanted to be able to drink. But I couldn't have any of these things.

So I told myself, and it gave me strength: NOBODY GETS EVERYTHING THEY WANT IN LIFE. YOU HAVE TO BE HUMBLE.

Bergen St.

F   G

I WILL NEVER DRINK AGAIN.

THE END